Animal eyes

TONY SEDDON

HODDER AND STOUGHTON

LONDON SYDNEY AUCKLAND TORONTO

British Library Cataloguing in Publication Data

Seddon, Tony
  Animal eyes. — (The Young naturalist).
  1. Eye — Juvenile literature
  I. Title   II. Series
591.1'823   QL949

ISBN 0-340-42657-8

Published by Hodder & Stoughton Children's Books,
a division of Hodder & Stoughton Ltd
Mill Road, Dunton Green, Sevenoaks, Kent. TN13 2YJ

This book was designed and produced by BLA Publishing Limited, East Grinstead, Sussex, England.

A member of the **Ling Kee Group**
LONDON·HONG KONG·TAIPEI·SINGAPORE·NEW YORK

Phototypeset in Britain by BLA Publishing/Composing Operations
Colour origination by Planway Ltd
Printed and bound in Italy by New Interlitho

Note to the reader
On page 59 of this book you will find the glossary. This gives brief explanations of words which may be new to you. Answers to questions are given on page 58

Contents

All about light

Seeing colours

Sunlight is made up of the different coloured wavelengths of light. When you look at a rainbow, you can see all these colours. We call these colours the spectrum. Light reflects or bounces off objects in its path. When we see an object we see the light that it reflects. A leaf appears green because it reflects green light. It takes in or absorbs all the other colours. A white dress reflects all the colours of the spectrum. This is why it appears white. Why does a piece of coal look black?

Wave after wave

Light consists of tiny packets of energy called photons. Bright light contains lots of photons. Moonlight contains only a few. There are no photons if it is completely dark. Light travels in waves like the ripples on the

surface of a pond. Each colour has its own special shape of wave. The distance between each ripple of a wave is called a wavelength. Every colour of light has a different wavelength.

▲ The Earth receives all its light and heat from the Sun, 150 million kilometres out in space. Light waves travel at 300 thousand kilometres a second. Can you work out how long it takes for light to reach the surface of the Earth from the Sun?

wavelength

Me and my shadow

Light travels in straight lines. This explains why you cannot see round a corner. It also explains why light causes shadows. If light cannot pass through an object, a shadow will be formed.

Animal shadows are tell-tale signs. They point to where an animal is resting. Because of this, many animals try to avoid making shadows with their bodies. They lie low against the ground. They sometimes press flat against a tree trunk. Some lizards even have flaps of skin along their sides. These act as shadow 'disguises'.

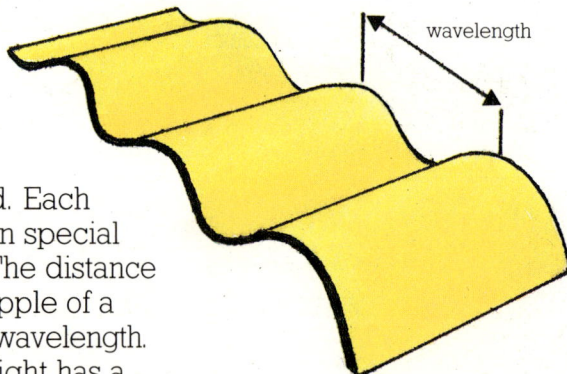

A glaring problem

Light is reflected from the surface of calm water. This makes it difficult for birds like pelicans to see clearly, or does it?

Diving birds seem to be able to cope easily with the bright glare. The brown pelican swims with its wings held open. They block out the Sun and stop glare from the surface of the water, so that it can see the fish below.

The umbrella bird

The black heron is even more skilful when it is fishing. It stands with its wings arched over its head, just like an umbrella. This forms a shadow and stops reflection from the water. The heron can now clearly see its prey swimming just below the surface.

▲ A pelican's eyes may work like a pair of sunglasses, with some kind of filter inside to cut out surface glare.

▼ The heron's wings make a circular shadow on the water surface. The heron always hunts for fish inside this circle.

Refraction and its problems

When light passes from air into another substance, it bends. This is called refraction. Have you noticed how the lines on the bottom of a swimming pool seem to bend in an odd way? It is very easy to see at the shallow end. This is another example of refraction. Imagine the problem diving birds like gannets might have with refraction. It could easily cause the bird to miss its target. Gannets solve the refraction problem by diving vertically onto their prey. Other diving birds do the same. In this way they make sure of a tasty meal.

More about ▷▷ The spectrum p 10 Moonlight p 32 Shadows p 52 Refraction p 41 Filters p 11

Many different eyes

Animals without backbones (invertebrates) form about 95% of all animal species. They include creatures such as insects, molluscs, worms and crabs, as well as corals, starfish, lobsters and squids. The simple and compound eyes of insects will be looked at later. Here we will look at the tremendous variety of shapes and sizes of eyes of some other kinds of invertebrates.

Simple eyes

The most simple 'eyes' are merely cells which are only able to detect light. Some invertebrates, such as mussels, no longer have eyes because the ability to 'see' is of no use to them. Incredibly, the young have tiny eyespots which they lose as they grow older.

▲ Each of the small brilliant eyes along the edge of the mantle of a scallop is only about one millimetre across. With these the scallop can detect the difference between light and shade, as well as movement.

An animal usually has eyes which suit its needs and way of life. Spiders have simple eyes around the head. These help them to spot approaching prey very quickly. The jumping spider has eight simple eyes of various sizes. When it sees an insect, it judges how far away it is with the outer pair of front eyes. Then it stalks its prey using the huge centre pair of eyes which give a clearer view of its prey.

The biggest eyes in the world

Some of the most efficient eyes must be those of the squids. They have two eyes, similar to our own, at the base of their tentacles. One of the largest squids ever recorded was washed up in

◄ The jumping spider has simple eyes all around its head which it uses to detect the approach of a flying insect. Imagine how useful it is to be able to see in all directions at once.

New Zealand in 1933. It measured 21 metres long and its eyes were about 40 centimetres across, the largest known eyes in the whole animal kingdom. It is possible that this was not the largest squid, and there may be even larger ones in the depths of the ocean. A squid's eyes are not only large, they are also very good at seeing fine details.

A squid may hold the record for the largest eyes, but scallops hold the record for the greatest number of eyes. A scallop may have between 50 and 200 metallic-blue eyes studded like fine jewels around the edge of its mantle. The scallop does not depend only on its eyes. It has many fine filaments around its mantle. These can detect movement in the water, and can warn of an approaching predator long before it could ever be seen.

▼ Rather than lie buried in the sand like a ghost crab, this purple shore crab hides among mangrove roots. So, it only needs eyes on short stalks, not long ones.

▲ The eyes of a squid are large and very efficient. They are very like human eyes, though the squid probably cannot see as much detail as we can.

Eyes on stalks

Some animals have eyes in rather unusual places. Crabs and snails may have eyes on the end of long stalks. The ghost crab, for example, spends much of its time buried in sand ready to ambush passing animals. Only its eyes protrude like a pair of periscopes to scan the beach for the next meal.

More about 〉〉

Simple and compound eyes p 12-13 Crab and lobster eyes p 21-23
Squid eyes p 43 Snail eyes p 21, 23

Colour vision in animals

Different wavelengths of light produce different colours. Everyone knows the red, orange, yellow, green, blue, indigo and violet colours of a rainbow. We call this band of colours the visible spectrum because we can see it. Humans have good colour vision, but they cannot see beyond the two ends of the visible spectrum. Some other animals react to non-visible light. Many insects and birds see ultra-violet light. Even more remarkable are certain types of snakes which can explore the world in infra-red light. They detect this light as heat.

Seeing ultraviolet

Although butterflies and bees have a fuzzy view of the world, their eyes are extra sensitive to ultraviolet light. This is very important to them. The colours that we see will look very different when seen in ultraviolet light. When a drab-looking butterfly with white spots opens and closes its wings, it doesn't look very spectacular to us. But to other butterflies, which are seeing ultra-violet light, the white spots appear as flashes of vivid blue. This is a much better signal for gaining attention.

Some flower heads also give off ultraviolet signals which are picked up by passing insects. Dull yellow flower heads form bright beacons to an insect's eyes. They work like the lights on an airport runway, helping the insects to make a safe landing on the flower.

ultraviolet light   visible light   infra-red light

◀ A spectrum showing the visible part, which we see, and the ultra-violet and infra-red parts, which insects and some snakes see.

▼ This is how a flower appears to our eyes. It is rather dull and not very exciting.

▼ This is a similar type of flower reflecting ultraviolet light. This is how an insect would see it.

◀ This rattlesnake uses its normal eyes during the day. At night it changes over to its other pair of 'eyes'. It has two pit organs which it uses to find its prey in the dark.

Coloured filters

Daytime birds not only display very bright plumage, they also see a greater range of colours than humans, including ultraviolet light. Their eyes also use another interesting method to detect different shades and colours. Each cone of a bird's eye contains a tiny oil droplet. The oil acts like a filter. It reacts to each colour of light as it falls on the retina. These filters are especially sensitive to orange, yellow and red. This is probably why flowers pollinated by birds usually have these same colours.

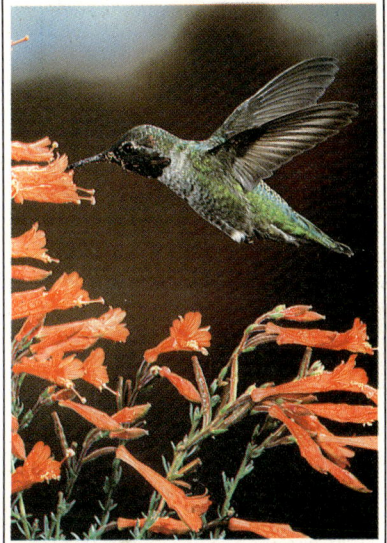

Red rag to a bull

Most mammals, such as cats, dogs, horses and cows, are 'colour-blind'. They see only shades of grey or perhaps very pale shades of colour. Their eyes are made to detect movement around them. It is not important for them to see colour.

You have probably been warned never to wander through a field with a bull in it if you are wearing a piece of red clothing. The colour red is supposed to make the bull angry so that it will want to charge you. But bulls are almost certainly 'colour-blind'. It will not make any difference to the bull what you wear. His eyes are tuned in to pick up movement. Rather than worrying about your red scarf, you should take more care not to stop and start suddenly, or make jerky actions!

'Seeing' infra-red

Infra-red rays are found beyond the red end of the spectrum. We cannot see them because their wavelength is too long, but we can feel them as heat. The rattlesnake pictured above can find a warm-blooded animal in total darkness by using the heat-seeking pits on the front of its face. It 'sees' the heat image of a mouse just as easily as we see it in bright daylight.

More about ▷▷ The visible spectrum p 6 Infra-red light p 31, 36-37 Filters p 7 Rattlesnakes and vipers p 36-37 Insects and flowers p 13

Insect eyes

The eyes of an insect are very different from human eyes. They cannot produce sharp pictures of the world around them. Many insects see in colour. Some see far more colours than us, whilst others see far fewer. Their world looks very different from our own.

Insects can have two types of eye, simple and compound. Sometimes both types are found on the same insect. The most basic type is called a simple eye. This is a small, rounded, clear lens which can only tell light from dark, and sometimes sees colours. It is found on caterpillars' heads or on the forehead of adult insects.

Compound eyes

The second type of eye is much more complicated. It is much larger and is called a compound eye. It is made up of hundreds of very tiny pieces placed together in a honeycomb pattern.

Each tiny portion of a compound eye is shaped like a long, pointed tube. The broad end of the tube reaches the outside of the eye and contains a clear lens. The thin end of the tube is joined to a special type of cell that turns light into electrical signals. Each different colour of light will produce a different signal. A compound eye sees the world as a jigsaw of tiny images. Each tube within the eye produces a tiny part of the overall picture.

▼ One compound eye of an insect can have from 10 to 30 000 sections, depending on the kind of insect. This picture shows the rainbow-coloured eyes of a horse fly.

Flower power

Insects which visit flowers for food need to tell one colour from another. Over millions of years, these insects have learned which colours lead to food. At the same time, flowers have developed patterns to attract certain types of insect. It is no use a bee with a short tongue visiting a flower with deep petals. The bee would be unable to reach the nectar. To avoid wasting time, the bee only visits flowers whose colour pattern it recognizes, and which it knows will provide food.

The lenses in the insect's compound eye cannot move, and so it cannot produce sharp pictures. The most that an insect can see is a fuzzy pattern of light, dark and colour. Many insects can only see an object if it moves, or if it is very close to them. A few insects, such as dragonflies or praying mantids, are very good at seeing movement and shape. Their eyes have up to 30 000 tubes, each seeing a tiny part of the complete picture. They depend upon their eyes to help them catch other insects as food.

Most adult insects have two compound eyes, one on each side of their head. Insects with simple eyes may have many placed in a ring or clumped together. The outside of all these eyes is made from a very hard substance. They do not need to be protected like human eyes. If you look carefully at a magnified part of a compound eye you will see lots of tiny hairs, knobs, or pits. These are special sense organs which the insect uses to smell, taste and feel. No other animals can do this with their eyes.

▲ A dragonfly has enormous eyes compared to the size of its body. On the same scale, a human would have eyes more than one metre in diameter.

▼ Hold the book away from you to see flowers as an insect with compound eyes might see them.

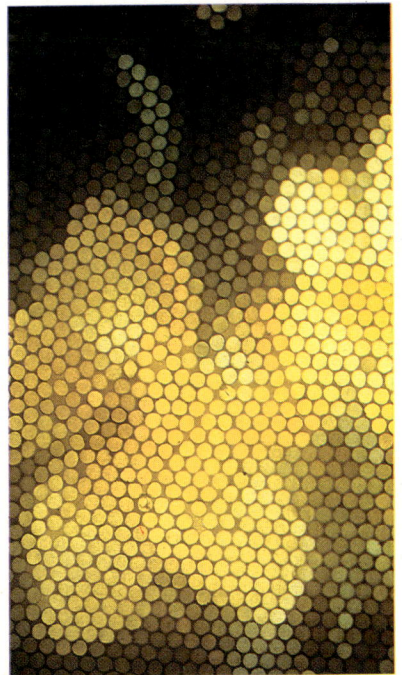

Our eyes

muscles (these move the eye)

cornea (transparent)

retina (lines the back of the eyeball)

eyelid

blind spot

iris

optic nerve

crystalline lens (cut away)

pupil

blood vessels

sclera (white of eye)

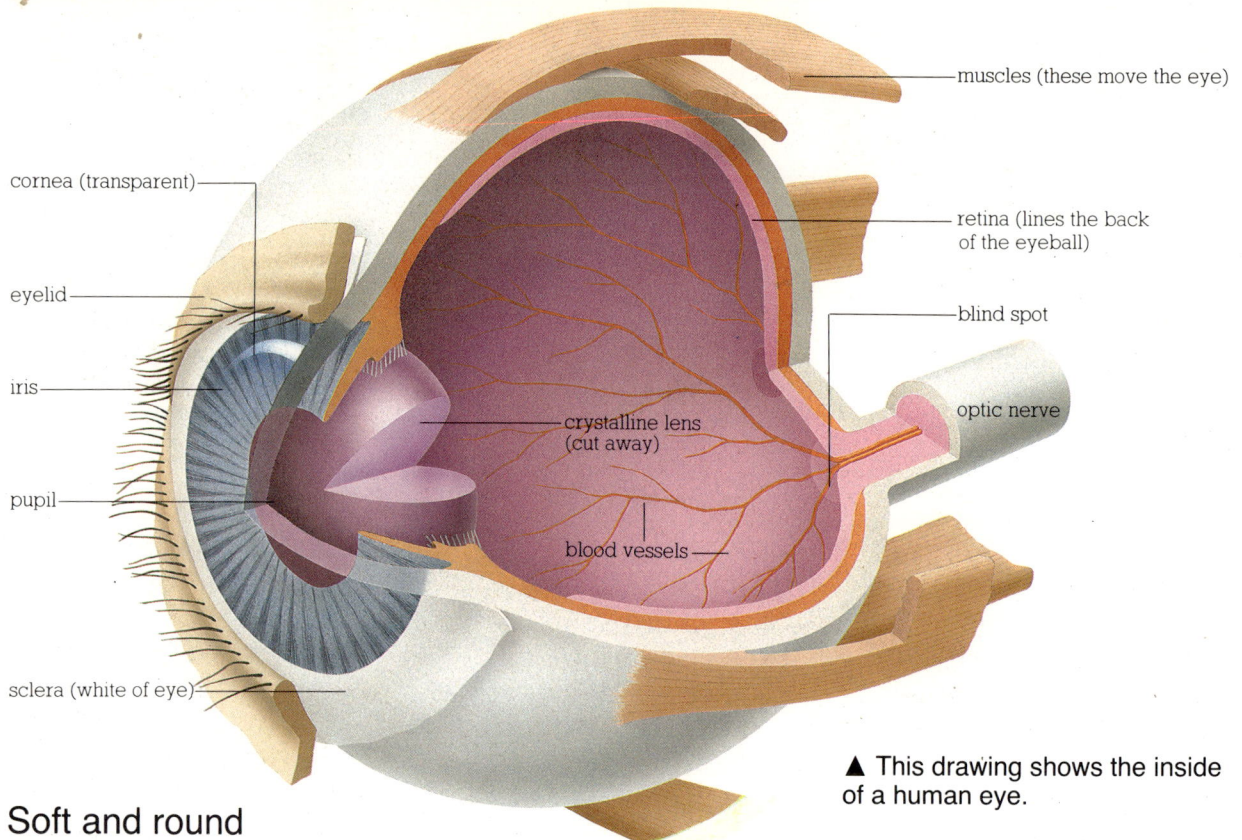

▲ This drawing shows the inside of a human eye.

Soft and round

The eyes are one of the most sensitive parts of the human body. By gently rubbing them, you can feel that they are soft and round. These features help the eye to work in the way it does.

Look carefully at your eyes in a mirror. Around the outside is a white layer, the sclera. This contains many blood vessels which bring food and blood to the eye.

Eyelids and irises

There are two eyelids at the front of each eye. Each has a fringe of hairs called the eyelashes which protect the

eyes from dust. The coloured circle is called the iris. When you say someone has blue eyes you are describing their iris. In the centre of the iris is a dark hole called the pupil. The iris controls how much light enters the eye through the pupil.

Eye make-up

Your eye works like a small camera. There is a film at the back of the camera on which the picture is made. Your eye has a kind of film at the back called the retina. This is where the light makes an image of what you see.

Your eye also has a lens, like a camera, and this focuses the light entering the eye on to the retina.

What's on the retina

The retina is made up of millions of tiny nerve cells called rods and cones. The rods respond to dim light for seeing at night. The cones react to bright light and colours. They are used for daylight vision. The retina collects the light signals and sends messages to the brain. The brain builds up these signals into a picture of the world you see.

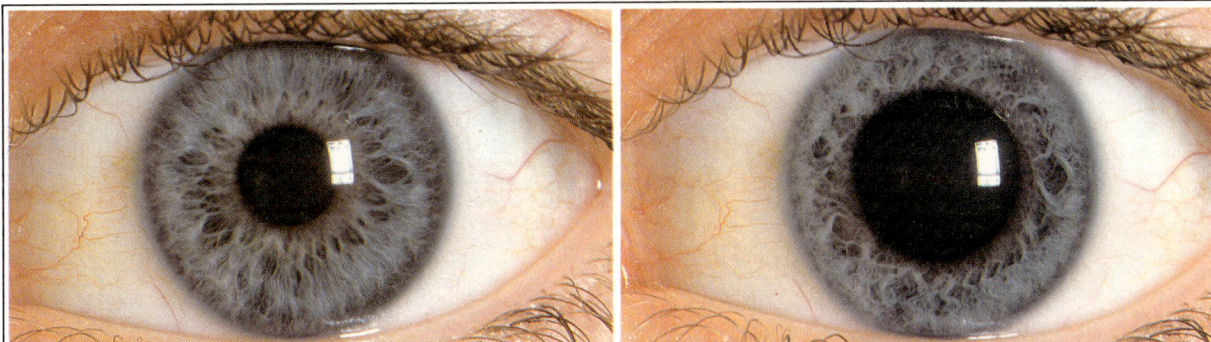

In bright light, the iris closes the pupil. Less light is now able to enter the eye. In dim light the opposite happens. Now the pupil opens wider and more light can enter. The iris is changing the size of the pupil all the time as the strength of the light changes. What do you think would happen to your pupils if you went out of a dark room into bright sunlight?

Sharp sight

Everyone likes to think that they have a 'sharp' pair of eyes. But how good is human vision? It varies from person to person. Some people have better eyesight than others. There is an average which the optician calls normal eyesight. There is a record of a young woman living in West Germany whose eyesight is twenty times better than average!

An upside down world

Did you know that you see the world upside down? Well *you* don't but your eyes do. The lens in the eye turns light upside down as it passes through. This means that the image which forms on the retina is also upside down. Your brain learns to change it back again. So you do see the world the right way up after all.

Taking care of the eyes

Our eyes need looking after very carefully, but they do have their own natural 'caretakers'. The eyelids and eyelashes protect them from damage caused by small bits of dust blowing into them. They also receive a good 'eyewash' every minute of the day. When we blink we wash the surface of each eye with tears. These keep the eye moist. They also help to kill any germs which get into the eyes.

▼ It is an upside down world on your retina (right), but you still see things the right way up (left). Your brain sees to this.

More about ▷▷ Eyelids and eyelashes p 18-19 The retina p 16-17, 25, 28-30, 32, 34-35 Rods and cones p 16-17, 25, 28-30, 32, 34-35 Experiments with eyes p 52-53

How we see colour

Not all animals see colours as we do. For many, the world is a place of shades of grey, rather like a black and white photograph. Other animals see their natural surroundings in very pale colours. They probably get a 'washed-out' view of the world which we find so bright and beautiful and full of colour. Humans have very good colour vision, as do our nearest relatives, the monkeys and apes. And the gaudiest animals of all, the fish and birds, probably see a range of colours beyond our imagination!

Rods and cones

In order to find out how colour vision works, we need to have a good look at the structure of the sensitive retina at the back of the eye. This layer is made up of millions of tiny cells, or light receptors, called rods and cones. You can see from the drawing that each gets its name from its shape.

▼ The retina at the back of the eye is lined with rods and cones. In the centre of the retina at the back of the human eye there are more cones than rods. These help us to see colours (see box).

Light falling on the retina passes through the outer layer of nerve cells to reach the rods and cones. Only about a quarter of the light entering the eye stimulates the receptor cells. Many light rays pass between the rods and cones and are wasted. Receptor cells which react to light are 'fired' to send signals, or impulses, to the brain. The rods and cones respond to different strengths of light. Rods react to low levels of light and are used for seeing in dim light. Cones are for daylight vision and for seeing colour.

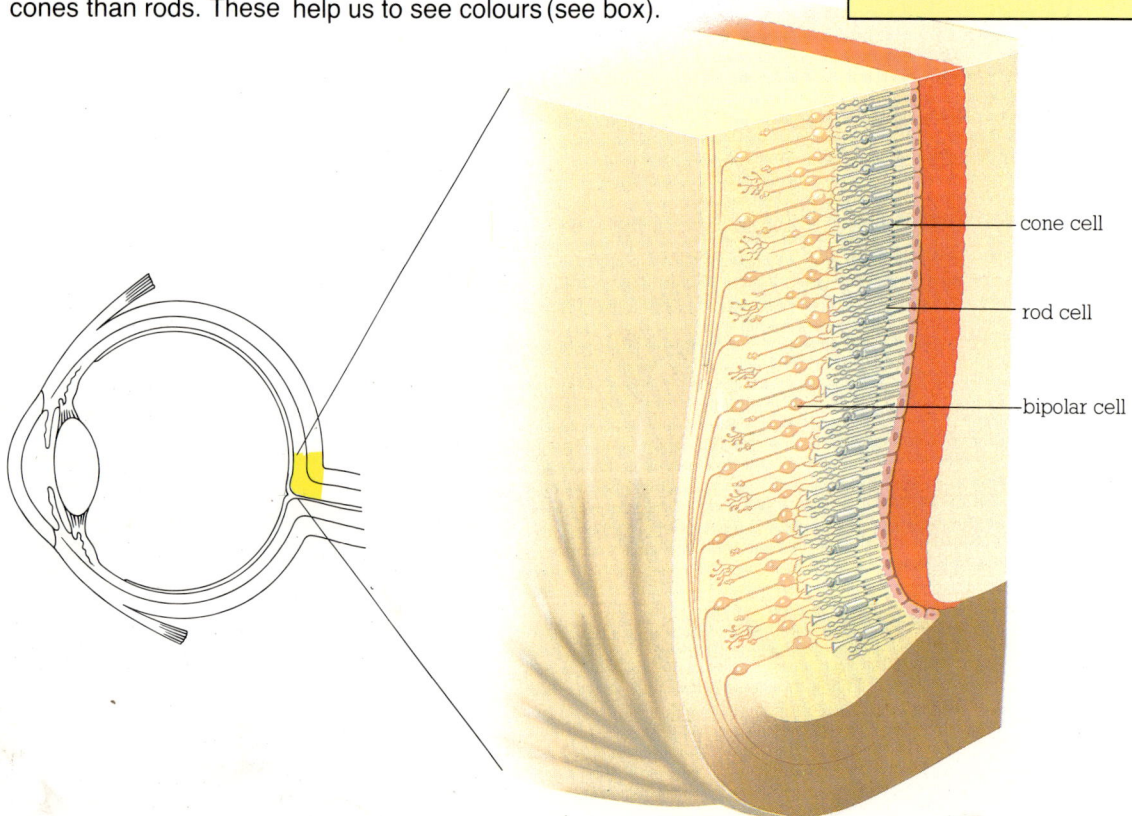

cone cell

rod cell

bipolar cell

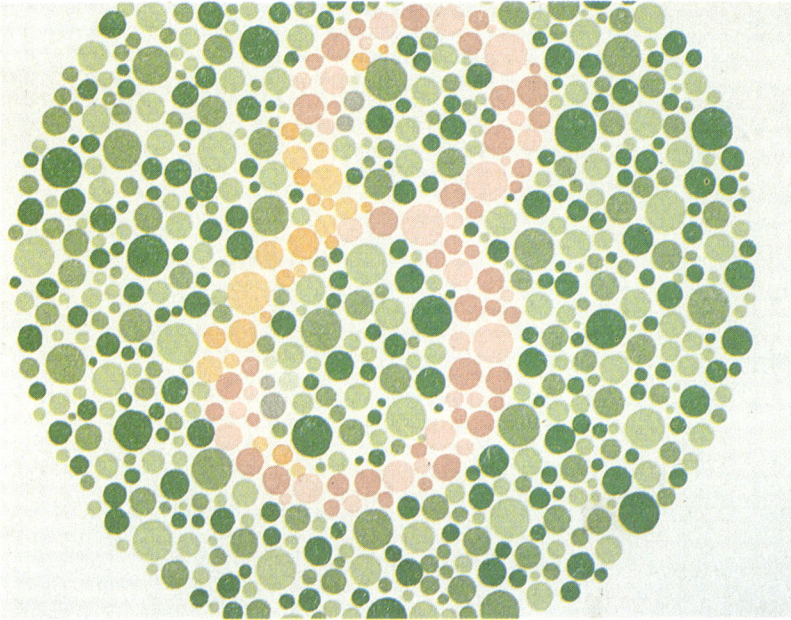

◄ Some people cannot tell the difference between red and green. They are red/green colour-blind. Are you one of them? Look at the circle on the left. Can you see a figure 8? If so, you have normal colour vision. Do you think being colour-blind affects a car driver waiting at the traffic lights?

Making pictures

We are still not sure how the brain 'sees' a coloured picture. Each cone may deal with one small part of the view the eye sees. Small groups of cones send their messages to a special cell, called a bipolar cell. The signals from these cones are then sent as a 'collected' message to the brain along the optic nerve. The brain translates the signals from the bipolar cells and uses them to build up a coloured picture of the original view.

It all works rather like a jig-saw puzzle, where each piece of the jig-saw is represented by a group of cones on the retina. Each bipolar cell unit will receive signals from only one piece of the retina. The brain then takes these pieces and puts them all together again to build up a coloured picture.

How do we see different colours?

There are three types of cone cells in the retina. Each type is sensitive to only one colour, either red, green or blue. These are the three primary colours. By mixing red, green and blue light in different ways we can make any other colour. When a coloured ray of light reaches the retina and 'fires' the nerve cells, the three types of cone break the light into the three primary colours.

More about Colour vision p 10-11 The retina p 14-15, 25, 28-30, 32, 34-35
Rods and cones p 14-15, 25, 28-30, 32, 34-35

Protecting the eyes

Eyes are the most delicate parts of an animal's body. They can easily be harmed. This is why they need to be looked after. Animals protect their eyes in many ways.

A bony box

Animals such as cats and dogs have a hard, bony skull which protects all of the delicate organs of the head. The eyes lie inside two holes called orbits. When looking at an animal's eye, only a small part is visible. Most of each eye is hidden inside the skull to protect it.

Eyelids

Animals such as birds and mammals have a small flap of skin called an eyelid above and below each eye. They are worked by tiny muscles which open and close them like a pair of small window blinds. They are the eye's protective shield. The lids can be closed very quickly if danger threatens.

Fish and snakes do not have eyelids. Instead, the front part of each eye is protected by a transparent layer. Fish and snakes cannot close their eyes.

Eyelashes

Mammals have a row of tiny hairs or eyelashes on the edge of each eyelid. They act like a protective fringe. Dirt and dust particles get caught in the tiny hairs. This stops them from reaching the surface of the eye where they might cause damage.

Cleaning the eyes

Mammals wash their eyes with a clear watery fluid called tears. Every time you blink you protect your eyes because tears act against germs. They also keep the eyes moist and stop them from becoming too dry.

Gecko lizards lick their eyes with their long tongues to remove dirt and dust. Some butterflies even have brushes on their small front legs. They clean their eyes with their feet!

Burrowing animals

Eyes are not much use if you spend all your time underground. Many animals which burrow either have no eyes to protect or only very tiny ones which are not difficult to look after. Some burrowing lizards have scaly coverings over their eyes. These protect the surface of the eyes from wear and tear by the sharp sand grains.

◀ A camel has extra long eyelashes to protect its eyes from desert sand storms.

The third eyelid

Some animals still have a proper third eyelid, the nictitating membrane, which can be pulled across the eye to give better protection. Many diving birds close off the third eyelid when they are swimming under water. It helps to protect their eyes and also helps them to see more clearly under water. Humans do not have a third eyelid. All that is left of it is the small piece of pink skin in the corner of the eye.

▶ This frog's eye shows the third eyelid pulled across. It has closed over the eye to give it extra protection. The frog can also pull its eyes into its head. In fact the orbits do not have a floor. There is nothing to stop a frog pulling its eyes into its mouth!

Eyestripes and eyespots

Many animals protect their eyes by disguising them or making them harder to see. Some do this by having stripes or lines across the eyes to break up their outline. Others have false eyes somewhere else on the body. These are often much bigger and brighter than their real eyes. False eyes attract predators away from the animals' real ones.

◀ The striped gaterin has an eyestripe which seems to run across the surface of each eye. This helps to break up the outline of the eye and so disguise it from predators.

More about ▶▶ Skull p 33, Eyelids and eyelashes p 14 Tears p 15, 45 Frog eyes p 21, 51 Eyespots p 48-49 Seeing underwater p 44-45

Eyes in position

Eyes to the front

A car has its headlights at the front. This is where you would expect to find them. They point the way forward. Many animals, such as lions and tigers, also have their eyes on the front of their head. But eyes are not always found in exactly this position in every kind of animal. Some animals even have eyes that change their position as they grow older.

► This kitten has big eyes facing forward. But are eyes always found in this position?

The fish with a roving eye

The plaice is a strange fish. It starts life off looking like any other fish. But, soon after it is born, its left eye begins to move. It gradually crosses to join the other eye on the right side of the body. Now the body of the plaice begins to flatten. When it is fully grown, it has the shape of a flatfish. Both eyes are on top of its head, looking up.

Up periscope!

A crab has two eyes on long stalks. They stick up like tiny periscopes. When a crab is hidden in its burrow in the sand, it can still see nearly everything that is happening on the beach above. When danger threatens, the two stalks are quickly pulled in to the safety of the burrow. Later, they are pushed gently out to have another look.

Snails also have eyes on long stalks called tentacles. There are two tentacles on the front of the head. Each one has a small, simple eye on its tip. The next time you come across a snail out of its shell, try a simple test. Very gently touch the tip of one of its tentacles. Watch how the snail quickly pulls its long tentacles in. Be careful not to harm the snail when you do this. The snail will withdraw its tentacles to protect its eyes from danger.

▲ This ray lives on the bottom of the sea. Its body is flattened as though it has been squashed by a heavy weight. It would be no good having eyes at the sides or at the front of its head. They need to be on top, looking up.

Above the waves

Amphibians like frogs have their eyes on the top of their head. Hippopotamuses and crocodiles have eyes in a similar position. All of these animals spend a lot of time in the water. They can lie hidden quietly beneath the surface but still see what is going on in the world above. A three-tonne hippopotamus is one of the biggest animals in the world. Yet it can lie, almost completely invisible, in its watery home and not miss a single thing!

◄ This frog can see everything going on around it even though most of its body is hidden beneath the water.

More about >> Fish eyes p 40-41, 44 Crab eyes p 8-9, 22-23
Snail eyes p 8-9, 23 Frog eyes p 19, 51

Eyes on stalks

Looking for movements

Crabs and shrimps have two large compound eyes similar to those of insects. Each eye is made up of thousands of smaller bits or units. Each unit is hexagonal (six-sided) or square in shape.

A crab's eye cannot see much detail. It gives only a fuzzy picture. But it is very good at picking up signals from sudden movements. It is these changes which a crab needs to know about. They are probably a danger signal from predators.

▶ The eyes of this ghost crab are at the ends of long stalks. In this position a crab gets a good view of the world around it. 'Periscopes' like this are useful if you live in a burrow, and want to see out.

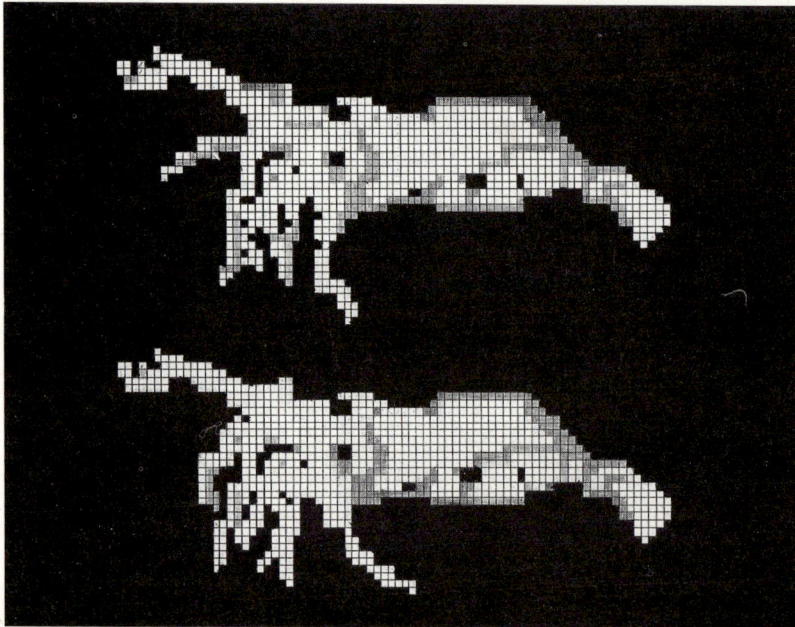

◀ Look at these two pictures. They show how a shrimp sees another shrimp. Can you make out a 'shrimp' shape in the pattern? Now look at the two pictures again. Can you see they are not quite the same. Can you see how they are different? How many changes can you see? Now imagine small parts of the pattern moving about. This is what a shrimp would see.

Lobster pictures

The surface of the compound eyes of lobsters and shrimps is covered in tiny squares. In the past people thought that each square worked like a separate eye. Now they think that each square sees only a tiny part of the whole picture. So a lobster's view of the world is like a pattern of tiny tiles. Imagine seeing the world through the eyes of a lobster! It would be difficult making out any details or even shapes. But if something moved, the pattern would suddenly change, and this would be easy to see.

Flag signals

Like all crabs, a fiddler crab has poor eyesight. It sees a very blurred picture. But this does not matter. A fiddler crab is always on the look-out for sudden movements, which may indicate prey or danger, and for signals from other fiddler crabs.

A fuzzy picture of a big claw waving about will signal to a male crab to 'watch out'. It may be getting too close to another male's feeding area. A female crab would be attracted to the same signals. They act as a flag telling her a mate is not too far away.

Snails also have their eyes on long stalks called tentacles. A snail's eyes are much simpler than a crab's eyes, and they do not give such a good picture. They tell the snail the difference between bright and dim light but not much more than this.

▼ Male fiddler crabs have an extra large claw. It is used as a flag to signal to other crabs. Even a crab's poor eyes can see these signals clearly enough.

Eyes of the hunter

The shape of an animal and what it looks like often tells you a great deal about its way of life. Many swimming animals have webbed feet, fins or flippers to help them move easily through water. Hunters often have powerful beaks, talons or claws. An animal's eyes can also give clues to the way in which it feeds and lives.

Eyes to the front

Although many animals depend on sensitive ears and an acute sense of smell when hunting for food, good vision is also important. Hunting animals normally have big eyes so that they can pick up light signals easily. Some predators also need to judge distance accurately when trying to capture a moving target. Because of this, the position of the eyes is important. Many hunters have their eyes facing forward at the front of the head. This gives

the animals binocular vision which helps them to judge distance more exactly.

Unlike other hunters, a chameleon moves its eyes independently of each other when searching for food. However, both eyes face forwards when it prepares to take aim with its tongue.

A preying mantis has two huge eyes on the front of its head. They can see both forwards and sideways. This helps the mantis to work out how far away its prey is.

◀ A chameleon is the only animal that can look forward with one eye and backward with the other at the same time.

▶ It is easier to judge distance when both eyes look forward from the front of the head. This allows the fields of vision of the two eyes to overlap. In the overlap area, the animal has good binocular vision because its brain is receiving information about the same scene from two slightly different viewpoints.

It's all in the retina

Not all hunters need to see fine detail to catch their prey. Many, such as hawks and eagles, do have remarkable vision. But others sense quick movements rather than see a detailed picture. This is enough to allow them to capture their prey.

The retina at the back of the eye holds the secret to how well an animal sees the world around it. It is the number and density of the tiny light sensors, the rods and cones, which control how well an animal sees.

Eyes on the horizon

Predators, whose eyes are always scanning wide open spaces, have an interesting adaptation to help in the search for food. The cheetah has a clear band of closely-packed cones in the middle of its retina. This provides a horizontal zone of extra sharp vision in the middle of its field of view. This is useful when searching for prey on the vast African plains. Birds living at sea, in deserts or other open spaces use a similar method for scanning wide horizons.

Birds of prey are the most skilled hunters in the animal world. They can spot a juicy meal from a great distance, and they often fly at high speed when making their attack. Hunting like this requires great flying skills and excellent eyesight. The peregrine falcon sees the world about eight times more clearly than we do. But sharp eyesight is not everything. Birds such as eagles and vultures use their eyes like a pair of binoculars, magnifying the ground below to see the finest details. Spotting a small mammal or a rotting carcass from a height of 100 metres or more is easy!

▼ The cones in a cheetah's eyes are packed together on the retina in a horizontal band. This is where the cheetah sees most clearly. In the photograph of the antelope herd, you can see that only the middle is sharply focused. This is how a cheetah would see the herd.

Wrap-round vision

A great many predators have forward-facing eyes on the front of the head to help them judge distances when trying to catch their prey. But eyes positioned like this give only a limited view of the world. They certainly cannot gather information about what is taking place on either side of the body or behind the animal's back. In order for this to happen, the animal either has to turn its head or move its body to face the other way.

▲ Eyes set on the side of the head give the European woodcock all-round vision.

Danger is all around

But just imagine being a predator's likely target for its next supper! Danger from predators is all around many animals. They are constantly threatened by attack from all sides. They need to spot danger signals quickly, no matter from which direction they come. Animals, such as antelopes, rabbits and zebras, need all-round vision to see advancing predators. They need a kind of 'wrap-round' vision so that they can see as much as possible at a single glance.

▼ This North American jack rabbit has large ears to keep it cool and large eyes that can see all-round to warn it of predators.

Sideways glance

In order for you to get a better view of the world around you, your eyes would need to be re-positioned. Look at the animals in these two photographs. Each one comes from a different part of the world and both face the possibility of ending up as a predator's dinner. Note how their eyes are placed on the sides of their head. In this position they give these animals a wide field of vision for all-round seeing.

All-round vision

Antelopes are able to get a complete view of their surroundings without moving their eyes, head or body. As the eyes are set on the sides of the head, they have only a limited amount of binocular vision. However, they do have excellent all-round vision. Now you can understand why predators, such as cheetahs or lions, have great difficulty in creeping up unnoticed on their prey.

one-eyed vision

binocular vision

Amazing facts

Animals, such as hares and rabbits, sometimes run into tree stumps or over cliff tops when escaping from danger. They are probably looking backwards rather than concentrating on where they are going.

Bulging eyes

If you have a pet rabbit or hamster, you have probably noticed its eyes seem to bulge out of their sockets. They give the impression that your pet is staring at you. This is because your pet's eyes are very steeply curved at the front, and this is true of all animals with a wide field of vision. The steeply curved front to the eye allows it to collect light rays from all directions. This gives the animal complete all-round vision.

▶ One of these fish is a predator on the other. Can you tell by looking at their eyes which is the hunter and which the hunted? You will have to imagine that one of the fish is staring down its long nose.

Super sight

If you think you have good eyesight, you probably find it hard to believe that it is possible to see the world much more clearly than you do already. But some animals do have much better eyesight than us. Birds of prey have the keenest vision of any animal. They see the world about eight times more clearly than the sharpest human eyes. A golden eagle has no difficulty in seeing a hare from a distance of two kilometres. Just imagine being able to see everything so clearly and in such detail!

central fovea

lateral fovea

direction of straight ahead viewing

direction of sideways viewing

field of binocular vision

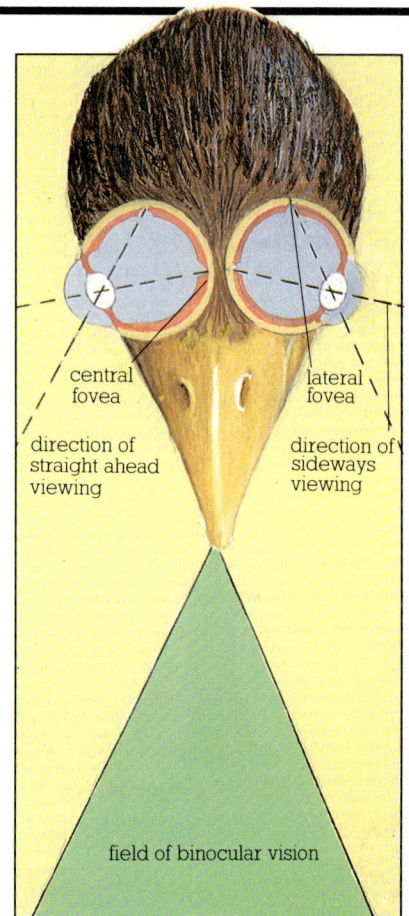

▲ All birds of prey have big eyes for letting in the maximum amount of light. The two eyes face forwards and sideways at the same time. Birds like this white-headed eagle have excellent binocular vision. This helps them work out how far away their prey is when hunting.

Apart from their large size, the eyes of birds of prey are unusual in other ways. For example, each eye has two spots on the retina where vision is very sharp. One spot is used for sideways vision and the other for straight ahead seeing. An object focused on one of these special spots, called fovea, is seen in much greater detail. Each fovea is lined with a great many cones. The fovea is pit-shaped and spreads the light out on to these very sensitive cones. This allows birds of prey to see things in detail.

The special case of the kestrel

Have you ever used a pair of binoculars? If so, you will know how important it is to keep them absolutely steady if you want to see clearly. Next time that you are lucky enough to see a kestrel out hunting, take a good look at it. When it hovers, its wing tips are moving too quickly for you to see, but it keeps its head quite still. This will give you a clue as to how a kestrel's eyes work.

A kestrel uses its special eyes for distance vision just like you use your binoculars. They allow it to see very fine detail and also magnify the scene below by up to three times. A kestrel hovering 20 metres above a field can spot a mouse as easily as we would a large cat!

▼ Even while it is hovering, the kestrel keeps its head still so that it has a sharp view of the ground below.

▼ Our view of a field from 20 metres above the ground.

▼ A kestrel's view of the field from the same height.

Super-sighted vultures

Vultures soaring hundreds of metres above the ground really do get a 'bird's eye view'. With their extremely sharp eyesight they can pick out details which we would find very difficult to see. Their eyes also magnify the scene below. This makes it easy to find even the smallest dead or dying animal. Very high-flying vultures use their built in 'binoculars' to spot low-flying birds which have found food. Then they simply drop out of the sky and play 'follow my leader'.

Amazing facts

In good light, a peregrine falcon can recognize a pigeon at a distance of more than one kilometre.

The retina in a buzzard's eye contains about one million cones per square millimetre of surface. This is about three times as many as is found in the human eye.

More about ▷▷ Binocular vision p 24-25, 32-33, 38, 47
Cones p 14-17, 25, 30, 32, 34-35

Night eyes

Rods hold the key

There is a layer of tiny sense cells at the back of each eye. There are two types called rods and cones. Cones are used for seeing in bright light and detecting colours. Rods respond to dim light. Nocturnal animals have many more rods than cones in each eye. This is why they can see better in the dark. But they will see a shadowy grey world. They will not see any colour.

◄ Compared to its body size, this tarsier has the biggest eyes of any animal. On the same scale, each human eye would be nearly two metres in diameter. The tarsier's pupils are so big that they cannot open up any more. Imagine the huge lens behind each pupil. These are a perfect pair of eyes for catching every bit of light on a dark night.

Big eyes

You might be suprised to learn that more animals come out to feed at night than during the day. This is because it is probably safer at night. However, there is not much light about after dark. Because of this, these so-called nocturnal animals need a special kind of eye. It must be big with a large pupil and a huge lens. Eyes built like this can collect every bit of light available. Most night animals probably see four or five times better than humans can in the dark.

▲ This nightjar has big eyes for seeing at night. During the day it depends on good camouflage to avoid predators. A bright pair of eyes would be a 'give away' to where it is resting. Because of this it keeps them closed until it becomes dark.

Eyes for 'seeing' heat

Rattlesnakes and their close relatives can see when it is completely dark. But they see in a different way. They see 'heat' pictures of objects with special eyes called pit organs. These can pick up infra-red signals from warm objects in their surroundings.

► This gecko lizard has very big eyes for hunting small insects at night. You can see that the pupils close during the day. Now each eye shows four small pinholes. Only small amounts of light can now enter.

The amazing oil bird

The oil bird from South America lives completely in the dark. It never sees the 'light of day'. It rests during the day in dark caves. At night it flies off to feed on fruit in the forests nearby. When it is inside its cave it does not use its eyes. It finds its way about like a bat. It sends out clicking sounds and listens for their return echoes. It is a kind of sonar system. Once out in the open, its big 'night-seeing' eyes help it find its way in the dark.

The cave dwellers

Animals which live in deep caves spend all their lives in the dark. Unlike the oil bird, they never come out, even at night. They live in total darkness all the time. Even the most sensitive eyes cannot work when there is no light. Cave animals have learnt to find their way about without needing eyes. Their eyes have gradually become smaller, and in most cases they have disappeared completely. They are blind. The proteus salamander is born with eyes, but they are lost as it grows older.

▼ Nocturnal hunters like lions have eyes which shine in the dark. There is a mirror-like layer at the back of each eye. It reflects light back into the eyes. This gives the retina a second chance to pick up any light it missed the first time.

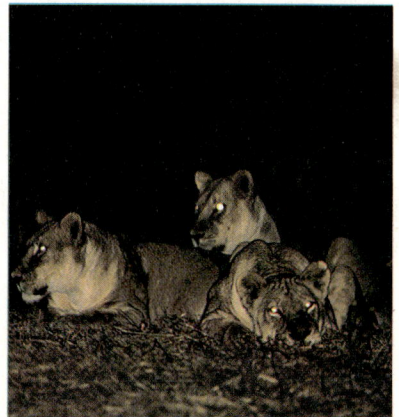

More about ⟩⟩ Night vision p 32-35, 37 Rods p 14-17, 25, 28-29, 32, 34-35 Rattlesnakes p 10, 36-37 Eyeshine p 34-35

Owl eyes

Owls galore

Most people can easily recognize an owl by its large staring eyes and its fierce expression. There are about 130 different kinds of owl spread throughout the world. They vary in size from the small pygmy and elf owls, no bigger than a sparrow, to the giant eagle owls, more than half a metre from beak to tail. Most owls have adapted to a nocturnal life, but some come out into the open and hunt during the day.

By the light of the Moon

Owls are the experts of the animal world when it comes to night hunting. They have many features which help them to live in a world of darkness and shadows, but it is their remarkable eyes which best fit them for a nocturnal way of life. No animal can see in complete darkness, but an owl can make do with the least amount of light possible. A barn owl can catch and kill a mouse in conditions that we humans would think of as being 'pitch black'. A tawny owl can find its prey in surroundings that are one hundred times darker than we can see in. How can owls perform these amazing feats of vision?

Rods by the million

The retina of all vertebrate eyes contains sensitive nerve cells called rods and cones. Rods are more sensitive to dim light than cones. An owl's eyes contain many more rods than cones – an adaptation for seeing in poor light.

Amazing facts

Many owls can see in light one hundred times less bright than starlight.

Most owls locate their prey by using their ears as well as their eyes. A barn owl can catch a mouse even when blindfolded.

◀ Look at this owl's face. Does it tell you that owls are night birds?

◀ An owl's forward-facing eyes give it good binocular vision because the fields of view from the eyes overlap. This, plus the enormous size of the eyes with their huge pupils, makes the owl an excellent hunter in moonlight.

binocular vision where the views from the two eyes overlap

Getting it right

Like all predators, owls have forward-facing eyes which give good binocular vision. Binocular vision is important for predators because it allows them to judge distance accurately. This is very necessary when an animal is seeking to catch another animal trying to escape. Have you ever tried to judge how far away an object is with one eye closed. Try it — you will not find it easy!

Big eyes

Owls have enormous eyes. They are so big that they take up most of the front of the skull. Most vertebrates are able to move their eyes using the special muscles attached to their eyes. But there is no room to fit any muscles in the eye orbit of an owl. So, instead of moving its eyes, an owl moves its head. It can do this because its neck is very flexible, so much so that the head can be turned through 180° on either side. An owl can look directly behind itself without moving its body!

▼ An owl's skull has two large eye sockets (orbits) to house the huge eyes. The bony wall that lies between the orbits is so thin that the eyes almost touch.

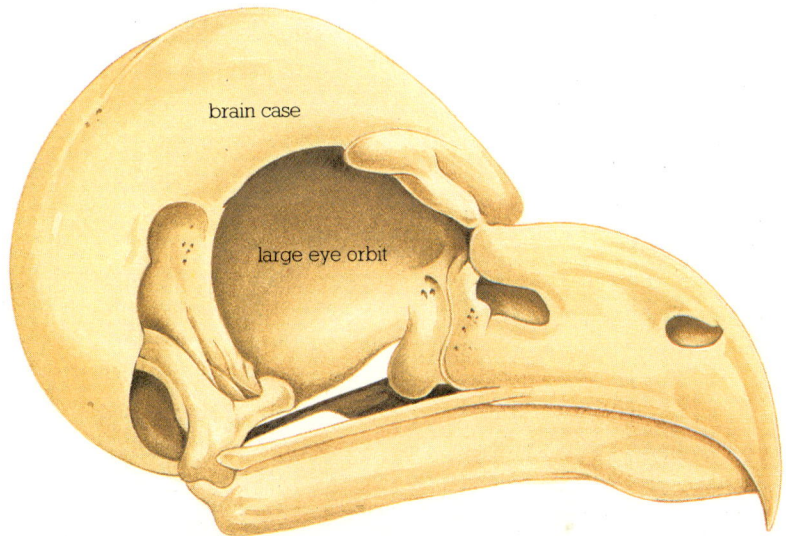

brain case

large eye orbit

More about Moonlight p 6 Rods p 14-17, 25, 30, 34-35 Skull p 18
Binocular vision p 22-25, 28-29, 38, 47

Eyes that shine

◄ The night vision of the African potto is improved by a special layer of cells, called the tapetum, behind the retina. This layer contains guanine crystals. Any light passing through the retina is reflected back by the mirror-like tapetum. This means that the potto can see at least twice as well in dim light as we can.

Eyeshine

Eyeshine is another adaptation to help nocturnal animals see. It allows better use of the small amounts of light available on dark nights. Light enters the eye and passes through to the retina at the back. Here it fires off impulses in the sensitive rods. However, not all of the light stimulates the retina first time round.

Nocturnal animals have a reflecting mirror, called the tapetum, behind the retina. This helps them to re-use any light passing through. It gives the light a second chance to act on the retina by bouncing it back towards the nerve cells. Animals with a tapetum see twice as well in the dark as those without one.

Cats eyes

Have you ever seen a cat's eyes shining in the dark? Motorists sometimes pick up a pair of shining eyes in the beam of their car headlights when driving along a lonely road at night. This reflection of light from an animal's eyes is called 'eyeshine'. It is sometimes found in fish, certain toads, crocodiles and snakes, and a few birds such as owls and nightjars. However, it is most common in mammals, especially those that are active at night.

Seeing at night is difficult as there is not very much light about. All nocturnal animals have more rods than cones on the sensitive retina at the back of their eyes. This helps them to see better in dim light as rods are very sensitive to poor light.

tapetum
rod cell
cone cell
light ray

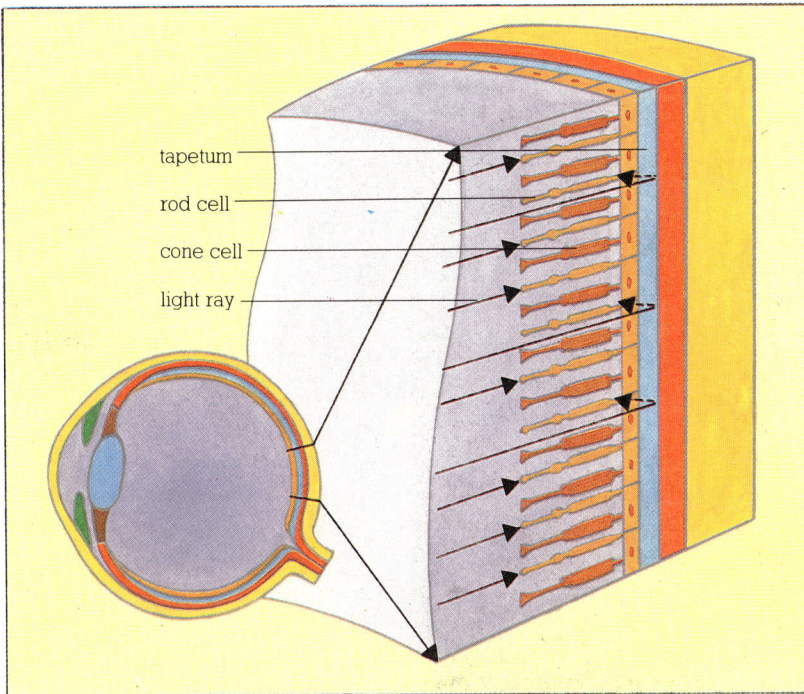

◄ This diagram shows the inside of the eye of a nocturnal animal. You can see the reflecting mirror, or tapetum, at the back of the eye.

▼ The douroucouli is a rare and unusual little monkey from the rain forests of South America. You can see that like all night animals it has big eyes and large pupils. It is the only nocturnal monkey and the only one whose eyes shine in the dark. This is further proof that eyeshine improves night vision.

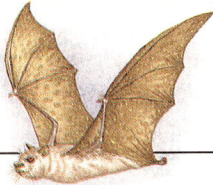

Eyeshine is common to all fruit-eating bats, but is absent from their insect-eating cousins. Such insectivorous bats have very poorly developed eyesight. Instead, they have developed an echo-sounding system, called echolocation, to help them navigate and find their food in the dark. The larger fruit-eating species do depend on vision to find their way about, so they need good eyesight for night flying. The mirror-like tapetum helps improve their night vision.

'Seeing' heat

▲ If you look carefully, you can see inside one of the pit organs of this eyelash viper. Can you see the thin membrane or skin at the bottom of the pit? It is this membrane which is sensitive to heat.

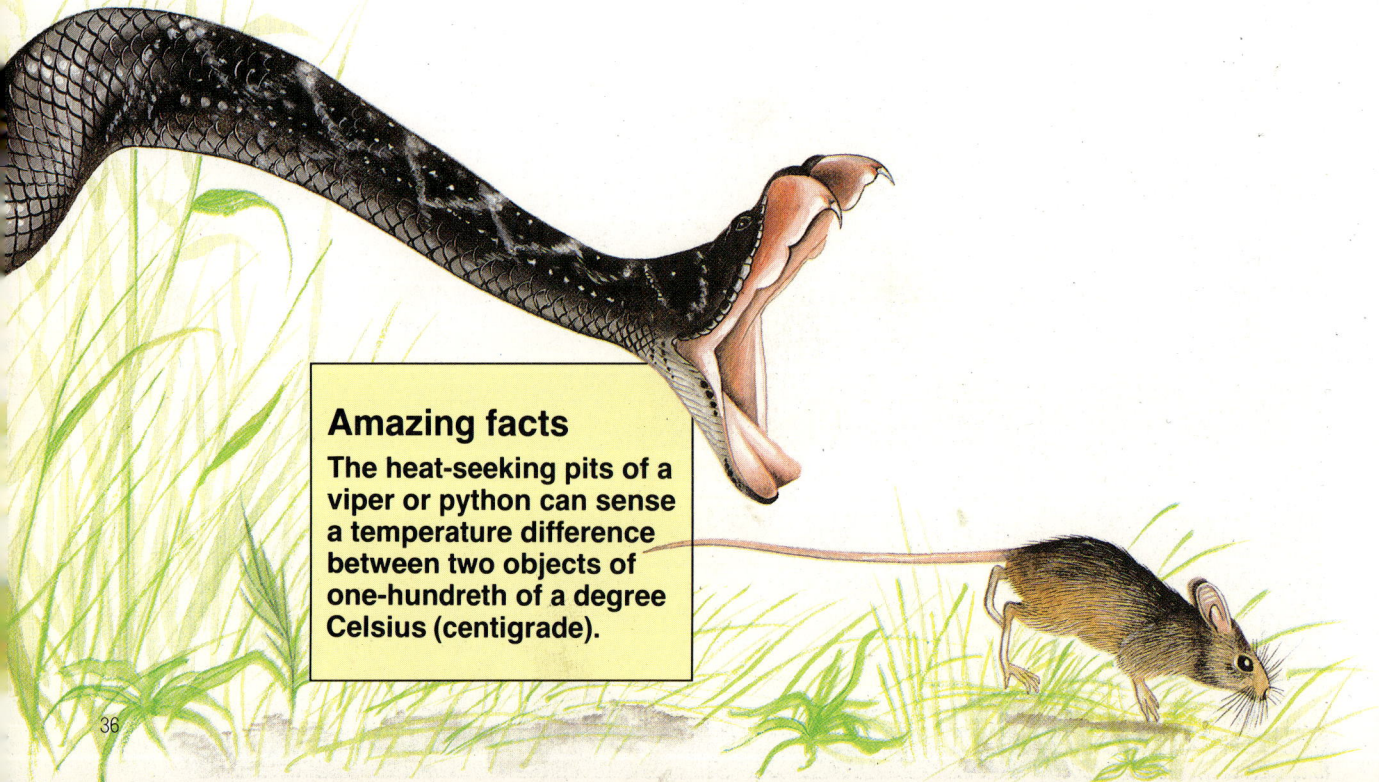

Amazing facts

The heat-seeking pits of a viper or python can sense a temperature difference between two objects of one-hundreth of a degree Celsius (centigrade).

Although many nocturnal animals can see easily in dim light, they are unable to use their eyes in complete darkness. When an owl is out hunting and the moon goes behind the clouds, its eyes are less useful. It would then depend on its highly sensitive ears to find its food.

Heat-seeking eyes

It is possible to 'see' in complete darkness, but you need special sense organs other than eyes to do the job. Some snakes, including vipers and boas, are able to catch their prey even on the darkest nights. They do this by picking up infra-red signals from warm objects including small mammals. As well as their ordinary eyes, which are used in the normal way, these snakes have a

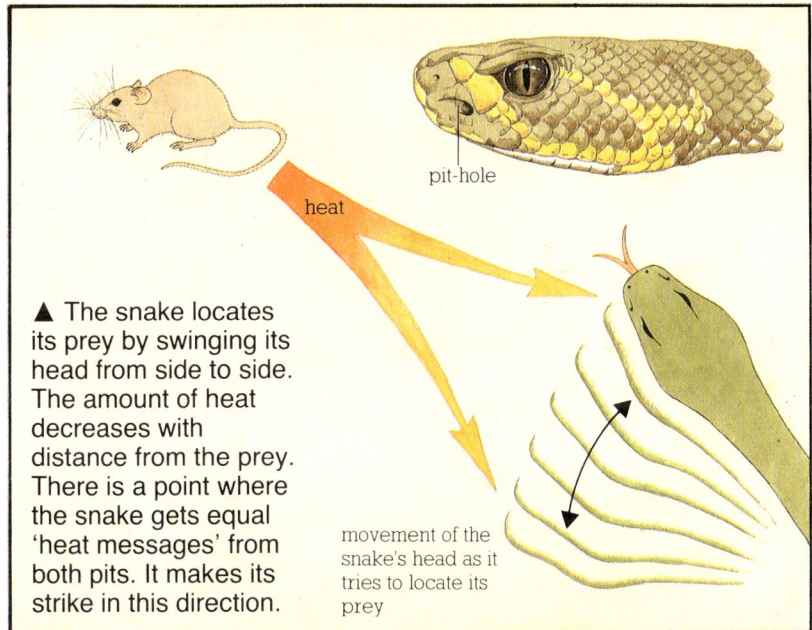

▲ The snake locates its prey by swinging its head from side to side. The amount of heat decreases with distance from the prey. There is a point where the snake gets equal 'heat messages' from both pits. It makes its strike in this direction.

movement of the snake's head as it tries to locate its prey

second pair of heat-seeking eyes, called pit organs. It is these which are sensitive to infra-red signals. They provide the snake with a simple heat picture of the area around it.

A rattlesnake's pit organs are the most sensitive heat receptors known in the animal world. Each pit contains a thin membrane behind which is an air-filled space. This membrane contains about 100 000 times more nerve endings than humans have on the same area of skin. Each nerve ending responds to infra-red heat coming from warm objects in the snake's surroundings. By using these heat-detecting 'eyes', a rattlesnake can ambush a mouse in the dark as easily as a grass snake captures a frog in the daytime.

◄ You are looking at an infra-red heat picture of a barn owl. It was taken with a camera containing a special film sensitive to infra-red heat. The film picked up heat coming from the owl's body.

More about ▷▷ Infra-red light p 10-11, 31 Owl eyes p 32-33 Night vision p 30-35 ▷▷

Wandering eyes

Two-way sight

Chameleons are unusual animals in many ways. Apart from being the quick colour-change specialists of the animal world, they also catch their food in an unusual and remarkable way. When a chameleon has tracked down an insect amongst the branches in which it lives, it shoots out a long, sticky-tipped tongue on which to catch its unfortunate victim.

This method requires a stealthy approach and a good pair of eyes. Chameleons have the strangest eyes of any animal, and their keen vision makes them very successful hunters. Their eyes are mounted in conical-shaped turrets. Each eye can swivel about freely in almost any direction. A chameleon is the only animal which can look both backwards and forwards at the same time!

▲ A chameleon can see two views at once, one with each eye.

▲ If the chameleon begins to look at just one object, the views start to overlap and finally it sees just one image.

Two views

A chameleon's eyes constantly swivel in their twin turrets as it scans its leafy world for a tasty meal. It has an unusual picture of its surroundings as it sees two very different views, one from each eye. But how does a chameleon's brain make sense of these two views? No one knows what a chameleon sees, but its brain may build up a picture from each eye in turn. It might even sample both views together. If both eyes begin to point at the same object, the two views begin to overlap. So, if one of the eyes spots a juicy insect, both eyes quickly focus on it. Now the views overlap completely. The brain in turn interprets one image as it is receiving the same picture from both eyes. Forward-facing eyes give good binocular vision which is important if the chameleon is to hit its prey with its tongue.

◄ A chameleon's eye muscles allow each eye to point 180° forwards and backwards. They can also look directly downwards and partially upwards as well. Only a fly that is perched on the top of a chameleon's head can possibly escape being detected by its all-seeing eyes!

Try being a chameleon

A chameleon's tongue is worked by a complicated system of muscles. You can imitate it quite easily. Perhaps you have teased or annoyed one of your friends at a party with one of the little devices called a 'blower'. It is a long, coiled tube of thin paper with a mouthpiece at one end. If you blow into the mouthpiece, the tube uncoils as the air enters it, rather like a chameleon's tongue. Of course, a chameleon uses muscles not air to work its tongue.

Set up some targets on a table, empty match boxes will do. Stand the boxes upright at different distances from the edge of the table, and then try to knock them over with your 'chameleon's tongue'. Is it easier to hit your targets with both eyes open, or is it better to take aim with one eye closed?

A sharpshooter's eyes

◄ When it spots its victim, the archerfish takes up its hunting position. Its body is completely submerged and its mouth is just touching the surface of the water. Its eyes are actually under water at the moment of 'firing', and this has puzzled many scientists. How is it that the archerfish is able to see from water into air? It seems to break all the laws of physics and what we know about the way light behaves.

A built-in water pistol

The archerfish is one of the most fascinating animals of the mangrove swamps of south-east Asia. It is quite a small fish, rarely growing to more than 20 centimetres in length. Its black and white striped body gives it quite a striking appearance.

Although it feeds on a variety of foods including microscopic plankton that float in the water, it has one remarkable hunting habit which makes it unique. It is the only animal that is able to kill its victim from some distance without having any direct contact. It's a kind of living water pistol, capable of shooting out a jet of water with deadly accuracy. Its aim is so good that it has no problem hitting a small insect target at a distance of two metres. It really is Nature's sharpshooter.

Practice makes perfect

The four-eyed fish does have special eyes for seeing in air and water at the same time. However, the archerfish's eyes are not like this. Its eyes seem perfectly normal for a fish. One interesting thing is that young archerfish have to learn to 'shoot'. At first, they are not very good marksmen and they have to practise hard before they become expert shots. This suggests that their eyes are not specially adapted for shooting from water into air. Even adult fish practise from time to time in order to keep their aim 'up to scratch'.

Light bending

Although light waves normally travel in straight lines, they can also bend. The left-hand glass is full to the top with water. The right-hand glass contains no water. You can see that the spoon seems to bend where the surface of the water meets the air. It is not really the spoon which bends, it is the light waves. This apparent bending of the spoon is called refraction. The spoon appears bent because the direction of the light is changed when it passes from water into air. Refraction always occurs as light passes from one kind of clear substance to another, such as from air to water or from water to air.

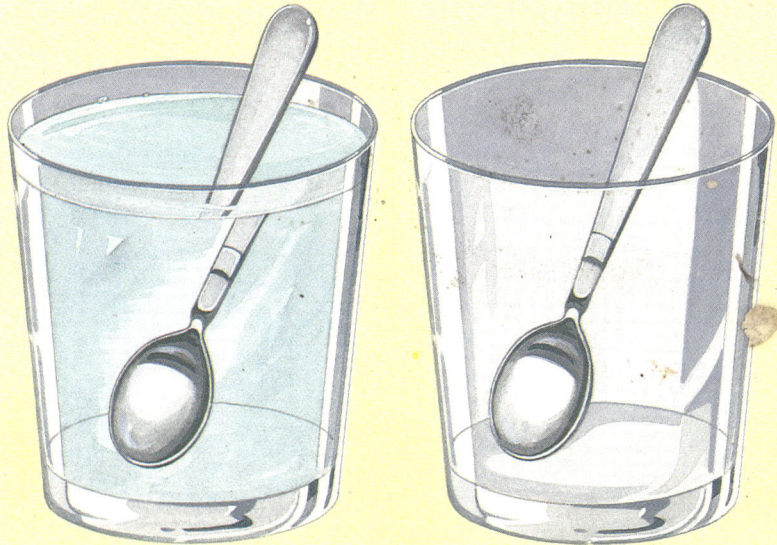

this is where the fish sees the insect when viewing from this angle

real position of insect

▼ If the archerfish 'fired' at an angle, refraction would make it aim the wrong way. Instead it 'shoots' upwards from beneath its prey. Now its aim is spot-on.

Up and under

The archerfish has very big eyes for the size of its body, and their size obviously helps it to find insects and other prey. But it is hard to explain how this extraordinary fish solves the problem of refraction. If a fish under water views an insect above the surface, the image will be distorted or changed as the light enters the water from the air. The archerfish has found a simple solution to the problem. It positions itself directly below its prey before 'firing'. Now there is very little refraction, and any slight error in aim is made up for by the power and spread of the jet of water.

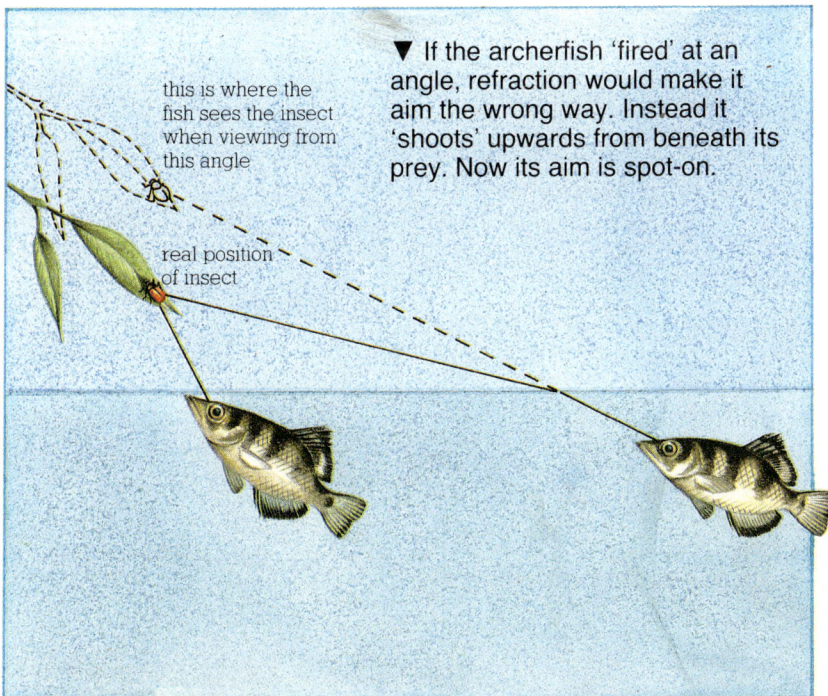

More about 〉〉 Refraction p 17
Seeing in water p 44-45

Monstrous eyes

Snails and many other animals without backbones (invertebrates) have eyes which tell them only if it is light or dark. Octopuses are similar to snails in many ways, except for their eyes. An octopus's eyes are most unusual and are very like human eyes. There is a lens, cornea, iris and sensitive retina. An octopus's eyes can focus and they can also control the amount of light entering. In bright light the iris closes to reduce the amount of light reaching the retina, and in dim light it behaves in the opposite way.

The biggest eyes on Earth

In 1860, in the middle of the Atlantic Ocean, the French battleship *Alecton* fought with a gigantic squid. The sailors on board estimated the weight of the monster's body (excluding its head and arms) at about two tonnes. The crew were unsuccessful in capturing the whole animal because the squid broke in two as they tried to haul it on board. As the creature's head and the attached arms sank beneath the waves, it carried with it what was probably the biggest pair of eyes in the world.

'Colour-blind'

As far as we know, octopuses cannot see colour. This is odd when you remember that they are the real experts at rapid colour change. They can turn from white to red in just a few seconds. How they do this when they are 'colour-blind' no one knows. Octopuses can also see polarized light. They can see the Sun and Moon even when they are hidden behind cloud. Perhaps they navigate by the Sun and Moon in the same way as birds.

Eye test

As its eyes are similar to ours, it is possible to give an octopus an eye test. Many hundreds of eye tests have been carried out on different octopuses. They have produced some amazing results. Here are some different pairs of shapes. Each time an octopus was shown a pair of shapes, it could easily tell one from the other. This is extraordinary when you compare it with its close relative the snail.

More about ▶▶ Eye structure p 14-15 'Colour blindness' p 11 Snail eyes p 8, 23

Seeing in water

Have you ever tried seeing under water? If you have, you will have discovered that our eyes do not work very well in a watery world. This is because they are made for seeing in air. If you want to get a clear view under water, you have to wear a face mask like the girl in the picture. Her mask traps a layer of air between her eyes and the water. Even though she is deep beneath the sea, her eyes are still looking through air.

A fishy business

Animals like fish, which spend all their time under the water, have specially designed eyes. Their eyes probably would not work very well on land.

▲ Without her face mask, this underwater swimmer would not be able to see clearly. With her face mask in place, she has a crystal-clear view.

A fish looks through a transparent covering over the front of each eye, just as we do. But this covering is a different shape from ours. It is much flatter, rather like the diver's face mask. This is the best design for seeing under water.

Have you noticed how a fish's eyes seem to 'goggle'. This is because a fish has no eyelids. It can never close its eyes. They stay open all the time even when it sleeps.

◄ A coral reef is the most colourful place on Earth. Many fish living there have excellent colour vision. Perhaps it is even better than a human's. The brilliant colours are important because they are used as signals between one fish and another.

Have you ever seen a picture of a brightly coloured shark? Sharks, and their relatives the rays, have no cones in their eyes. They cannot see colours, so a bright and colourful world is not important to them. This is why most sharks and rays are dull grey, brown or green in colour.

Big whales don't cry

Even though whales and seals are mammals, they have 'fishy' eyes. The front cornea is flattened just like a fish. Again it is designed like the diver's mask for good underwater viewing.

The outer covering of a whale's eye is much thicker than ours. This is probably because many whales are deep-sea specialists, often diving down hundreds of metres below the surface. A whale's eyes have to stand up to enormous pressures. If they did not have a thick, tough outer covering they would be squashed flat by the weight of the water.

Whales don't cry. They have no tear glands in their eyes. But then they do not need tears. Their eyes are bathed in water all the time.

It's a dull world

Living under water can be a very dull business. The light quickly disappears as you go deeper. Many animals have special devices to help use all the light available. Whales and seals even have a reflecting layer at the back of their eyes. It works like the 'mirror' found in the eyes of many nocturnal animals. The retina of whales' eyes also contain mainly rods with very few cones.

▲ The four-eyed fish is really odd. It is the only fish which can see above and below water at the same time. Each eye is divided into two parts. The top part looks up into the air. The bottom half looks down into the water below.

▼ The whirligig beetle makes its home at the meeting place of air and water. Each compound eye is divided into two parts. The top half sees above the surface of the water. The bottom part is for underwater viewing.

More about >> Fish eyes p 40-41, 46-47 Light and water p 46 Tears p 15, 18 Nocturnal vision p 30-37

Deep-sea eyes

The world's oceans can be divided up into different layers or zones. There are surface waters and deep water zones with a mid-water layer in between. The surface waters are lit well enough by sunlight to allow the eyes of the animals living there to work perfectly normally. However, in the twilight or mid-water zone, and in the deep parts of the ocean, it is a different story.

Only specially adapted eyes can see in the dim light of the twilight zone. At greater depths, eyes are of no use whatsoever because there is not enough light to see by. Animals that live in the deepest parts of the oceans have small eyes or no eyes at all. Instead, they rely much more on taste, touch and smell to find out more about the world around them.

▼ The lantern fish is a typical inhabitant of the twilight zone. Can you say what advantage it gains by having large, upward-looking eyes?

Fading colours

Sunlight is a mixture of colours which we call the visible spectrum. Each colour has its own wavelength. As sunlight filters down through sea water, some of the colours are absorbed more quickly than others. This is why sea animals appear to be different colours at various depths. Red is the first colour to disappear, then yellow and finally blue. A fish which appears red to our eyes at the surface, seems to change colour as it swims deeper. Below 150 metres it seems to have no colour at all — it appears to be black.

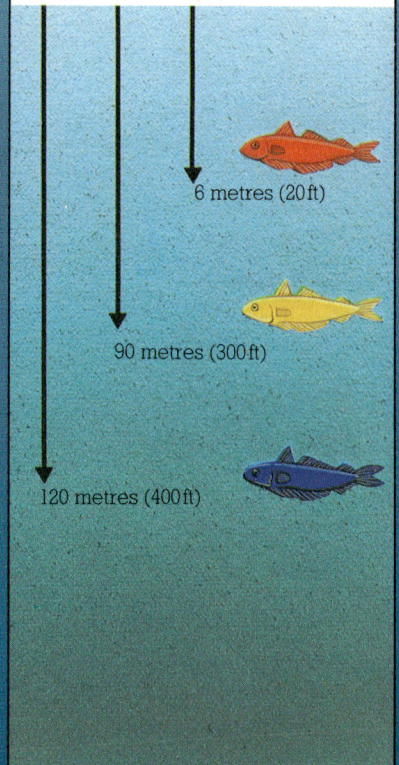

6 metres (20 ft)

90 metres (300 ft)

120 metres (400 ft)

The twilight zone

Fish living in the twilight zone, between 200 and 6000 metres below the surface of the sea, have very sensitive eyes. They are, perhaps, the most sensitive eyes in the animal kingdom. They are certainly able to make most use of the very faint light which manages to reach the twilight zone.

Most vertebrate animals' eyes are shaped like a ball. Deep-sea fish have tube-shaped eyes rather like an owl's, but they may be even better than an owl's eyes for seeing in poor light. They are different from other types of eye because each eye has two sensitive retinas.

One receives images from distant objects in front of the fish. The other is for looking upwards and for seeing things close up.

Deep-sea fish are mainly predators, so good eyesight is important for finding food. They also need to be able to judge exactly how far away their prey is. Their tubular eyes help them do this.

▼ Note how the eyes of the hatchet fish stick up out of the head like miniature telescopes. They provide it with good vision in the dark waters in which it lives.

Eyelights

Many deep-sea animals produce their own lights to help in camouflage and to enable them to see better in the dark water. These lights are produced by pockets of bacteria which the animals can switch on or off. Flashlight fish have their lights around their eyes. When turned on, they light up the scene in front and above. Small shrimps and other creatures get caught in the beam from these 'headlights' and make easy targets for a meal.

Fish eyes p 40-41, 44-45 Owl eyes p 32-33 Light and water p 45
Predator eyes p 24-25

More about

Eyespots and false eyes

'Eyes' are not just for seeing. Some animals, including fish, insects and amphibians, use eye patterns for other things. Butterflies are usually so brightly coloured that they appear to be offering up themselves as a delicious titbit for every animal looking for a snack. Apart from being brilliantly coloured, many butterflies are also slow moving and generally quite defenceless — or are they?

Shock tactics

Some butterflies have found a way to shock or frighten away a would-be attacker. The answer lies in the eyes, but not the usual kind. Big, round, frightening eyespots are the secret. Tucked away on the hind wings, they make a good defence mechanism when suddenly displayed. They certainly help to prevent some butterflies being eaten.

Heads or tails?

Some butterflies like this one from Brazil have two heads, or at least this is what it seems. In fact they have developed a false head at the back of the hind wings. It even has make-believe antennae and false eyes. The effect is to puzzle an attacking bird. The predator is even more baffled when the butterfly seems to take off backwards!

◄ This big caligo butterfly lives in the rain forests of South America. It has two huge eyespots underneath each hind wing which are normally kept out of sight. But if attacked, it rolls over on the twig it is resting on, and displays a scary face. This insect is also called the owl butterfly. Can you guess why? If not, turn the page upside down and look again.

Snakes alive!

Caterpillars are also in constant danger so they too use eyespots as a means of defence. The puss-moth caterpillar can pull in its head, leaving a false face and large 'eyes' to scare away a predator. If this trick does not work, it can squirt its attacker with a jet of formic acid.

The hawk-moth caterpillar pretends to be a snake when attacked by a predator. It blows up the front part of its body to look like a snake's head. The two false eyes complete the picture. The caterpillar even hisses and threatens to bite like a snake.

▲ Would you be frightened off by this false-eyed frog's staring bottom?

▼ If you were a predator, which end of this fish would you attack? If it is its 'eyes' which attract you, you would probably go for the wrong end!

Bottoms up!

Imagine having a pair of 'eyes' on your bottom. It certainly would give you a rear view! In fact, no animal has eyes on its rump, but the South American false-eyed frog has two large eyespots placed firmly on its posterior. When the frog is threatened, it puffs itself up and faces its attacker with its bottom. The predator suddenly finds that its frog prey has become a fierce face with two huge staring eyes. It is enough to frighten away any predator.

An 'eye' in the tail

The golden long-nosed butterfly fish has a big eyespot near its tail. This form of camouflage lures attackers away from the fish's head. This fish spends much of its time paddling backwards to give the impression that its false eye is at the front of its body. Attackers usually get only a mouthful of water or a piece of tail as the fish darts away in the 'wrong' direction.

More about 〉〉 **Eyestripes and eyespots p 19**

Eyes do other things

◄ No one knows why a horned-toad squirts blood from its eyes. It probably frightens off an attacker but there may be other reasons as well. The sight of blood may trick an enemy into thinking the lizard is injured. Or it may be that the sprays of blood have nothing to do with defence.

▼ Female turtles living at sea have to come ashore to lay their eggs. They often have to travel long distances to find a quiet beach where their eggs can develop undisturbed.

Blood squirter

The horned-toad is really a small lizard from the hot deserts of North America. It sometimes behaves in a very unusual way. It squirts blood from the corner of the eyes. Some people think that the blood is caused by parasites which live in the eyes.

There is a small eyelid above each eye which swells up with blood if the lizard suddenly becomes scared. It quickly swells to bursting point. Then the blood comes out in a long spurt. Beware if you get too close to a resting horned-toad. Its aim is very accurate. It has no difficulty in hitting a target as much as a metre away.

Crying turtles

Sea turtles feed mainly on fish. They take in a lot of salt with their food. Too much salt is harmful to a turtle so it has to find a way of getting rid of the salt it does not want.

Turtles have a special little bag near the corner of each eye. It is called a salt gland. This small gland passes the unwanted salt into the corner of the turtle's eye. The turtle then produces tears to wash the salt away. Perhaps the turtle's tears also wash away any sand grains which get into its eyes as it crawls up the beach to lay its eggs.

Even some sea birds like penguins and albatrosses seem to cry. But the tears are not from their eyes. Sea birds get rid of their extra salt through their nose.

▲ When it is chewing its food a frog's eyes keep disappearing. They go in and out of its mouth.

▼ The saltwater crocodile is the biggest reptile in the world. It also has problems with too much salt. Like turtles, crocodiles get rid of their unwanted salt by crying. Perhaps this is what is meant by 'crocodile tears'.

Eyes for feeding

If ever you get a chance to see a frog eating, watch what it does with its eyes. They seem to do a disappearing act every time it swallows. A frog can almost swallow its eyes, but not quite. It uses them to hold bits of food in its mouth. They also help squeeze the food towards its throat. A frog really can pull its eyes into its mouth when it needs to. That is why they seem to keep disappearing.

More about ⟫ Frog eyes p 19, 21
Crocodile eyes p 21

Things to do with eyes

Everybody's a little blind

One part of the retina in your eye has no rods or cones. It is where the nerve leaves the eye to go to the brain. This area is called the blind spot.

●   ✛

1. Close your left eye.
2. Stare at the circle with your right eye.
3. Move the page forwards and backwards until the cross disappears.

When the cross vanishes its image is falling on the blind spot of your right eye. This is why you cannot see it.

Closing time

You will need a torch and a mirror for this.

1. Stay in a dark room for two minutes.
2. Hold the mirror in front of your face.
3. Shine the torch on your eyes.
4. Watch what happens to your pupils.

You will see them get smaller but you will have to look quickly. When you were in the dark, your pupils opened wide to let in more light. As soon as you shine the torch into your eyes, the pupils become smaller to cut down the amount of light entering your eyes.

Two eyes are better than one

Try this experiment with a friend. You will need a cup and a small coin.

1. Put the cup on the table and stand about 3 metres away.
2. Cover your left eye with your hand.
3. Ask your friend to hold out the coin above the cup but a little in front of it.
4. Keep your one eye on the cup and the coin and ask your friend to move his hand until you think it is directly above the cup.
5. When you think his hand is in the correct position tell your friend to let go of the coin. How good a 'shot' are you?
6. Now try with both eyes open. Does your aim improve?

The floating 'sausage'

1. Hold your index fingers about 2 cm apart with the tips pointing towards each other.
2. Now look just above them and focus on a distant object.

Can you see a 'sausage' floating between your finger tips? Each eye is seeing a slightly different view of your two finger tips. This is why you see the floating 'sausage'.

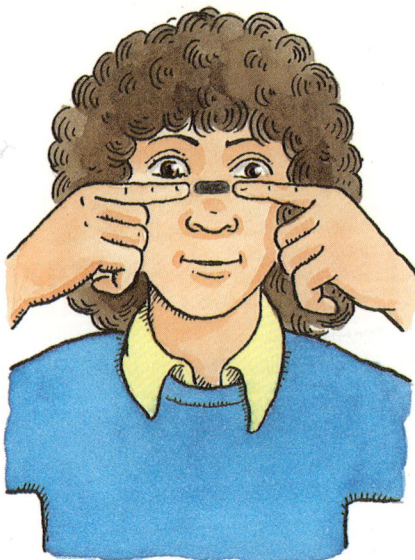

Everyone's one-eyed

Did you know you use one eye more than the other? Everybody has a dominant eye. It all depends if your brain is right- or left-sided.

1. Keep your right eye closed and point at a distant object with your index finger.
2. Make sure your left eye is lined up with what you are pointing at.
3. Now open your right eye. If your finger moves to the left your right eye is dominant.
4. To check your results repeat the experiment with your left eye closed.

Upside down world

The image on your retina is always upside down. But your brain learns to turn it back the right way up again. Everything seems to be normal. Here is how you can prove that eyes really do 'see' the world the wrong way up.

1. Make four small holes close together in a piece of paper.
2. Hold the paper about 10 cm from your right eye. You will need to hold the paper between your eye and a bright light. A window will do.
3. Hold a pencil point upwards. Move it very carefully towards your right eye. You will need to bring the tip of the pencil almost up to your eye. BE CAREFUL not to poke the pencil in your eye. Ask a friend to help you. She can shout a warning if the pencil gets too close.

Explanation

Narrow beams of light pass through the small holes on to the retina of your right eye. They cannot pass through the pencil point so it appears as a shadow on the retina. But you see the shadow of the pencil tip upside down. You have proved that an image falls upside down on your retina. Your eyes really do 'see' the world the wrong way up.

Feeling the strain

1. Hold this page about 20 cm from your eyes.
2. Focus on one word and keep looking at it.
3. Slowly bring the page towards you. Try to keep the word in focus.

Can you feel your lenses change shape as they try to focus on the word? Do not bring it too close or you may strain your eyes.

A hole in your hand

1. Roll a sheet of paper into a tube.
2. Hold the tube to your right eye like a telescope.
3. Hold your left hand in front of your left eye. You will need to hold it about 10 cm away.

If you get everything in the right position, you will see a big 'hole' in your hand. This is because two eyes are producing a confusing picture for your brain to work out.

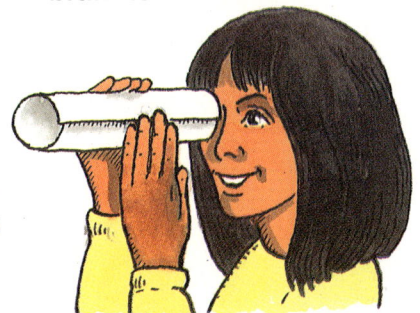

Seeing is not believing

When you look at an everyday object, such as a teacup, you have no difficulty in recognizing it. This is because you have seen the same kind of object many times before. Even if you see the teacup from an unusual view, you will probably recognize it fairly easily. You do this by using your imagination to compare the cup's shape with that of other cups that you have seen. By doing this you slowly build up a picture of the cup which your brain is able to recognize. This important link between seeing and memory is called perception.

When we are very young we have to learn how to use our eyes. At first, we are unlikely to make much sense of the world around us. But gradually we begin to recognize things. As we get older, we come to expect that our perceptions will be right. So, for example, we can eventually recognize a teacup even if we cannot see it. We can identify it by touch and feel. Again, we use our imagination. But sometimes we get a very confusing picture, and then we are not sure what we see. Two people can look at the same object and see entirely different things.

▲ Do you see a vase or a sideways view of two people looking at each other? Can you switch from one to the other?

▲ You probably see here an ugly old witch. Are you surprised to learn that some people interpret this as a picture of a young girl?

In or out, up or down
Are you looking down into the box from above, or are you viewing it from the front? With practice you can see both views by switching from one to the other.

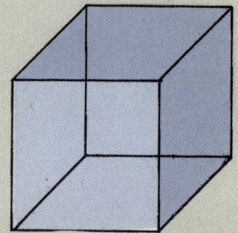

Try these stairs. Do you think you could walk up or down them? Or are you viewing the staircase from underneath?

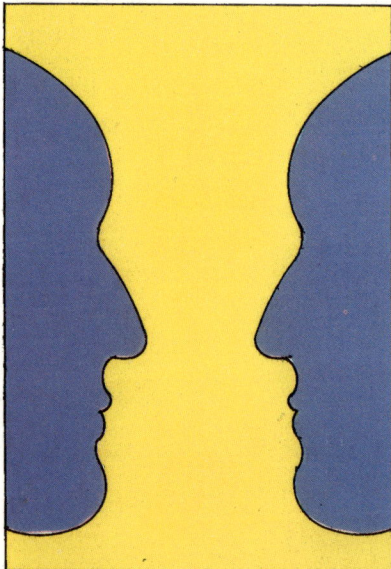

► Here are some well-known optical illusions. Is what we think we see really there? (A) Do the two red lines really bend? (B) Are the square and circle really square and circular? (C) Which needle has passed through the eight horizontal lines? (D) Surely the line on the left is shorter than the line on the right. (E) Are the two horizontal lines the same length, or is one shorter than the other? Make your guess then check all your answers with a ruler.

E

B

D

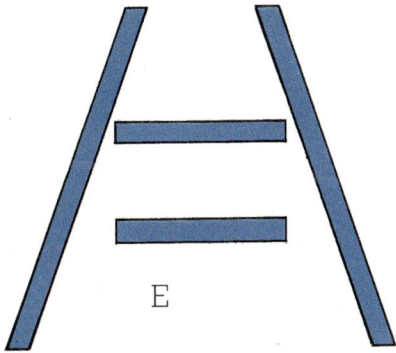

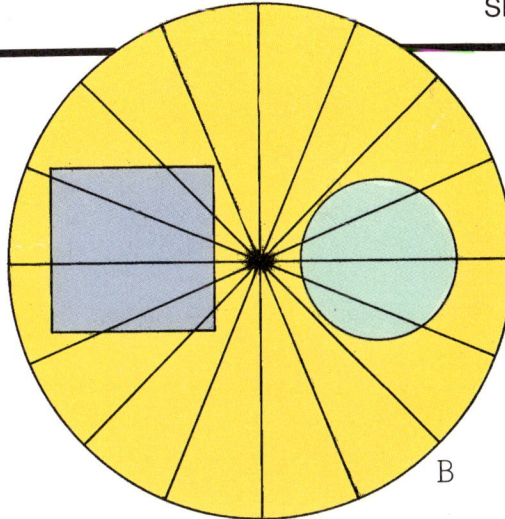

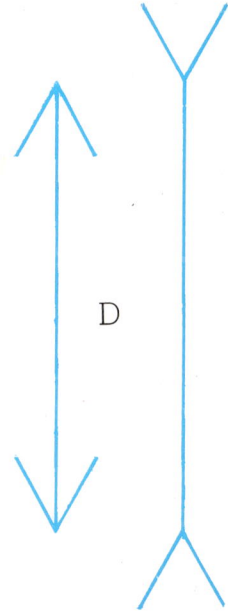

▼ This is not an optical illusion, but try it. Stare at the black dot for one minute. Then look at a piece of white paper. Whose famous face do you see?

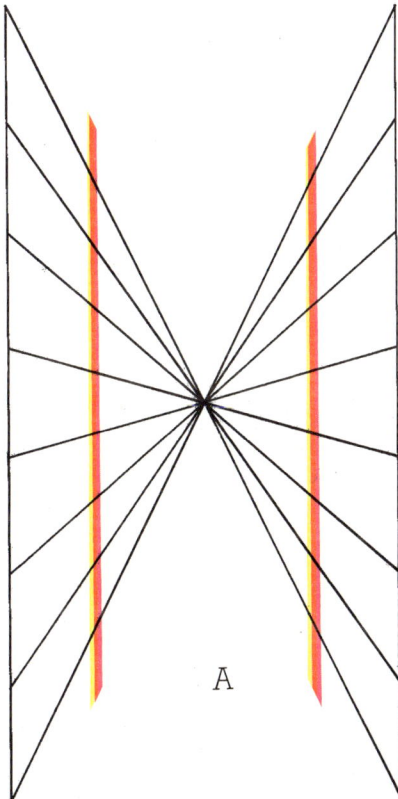

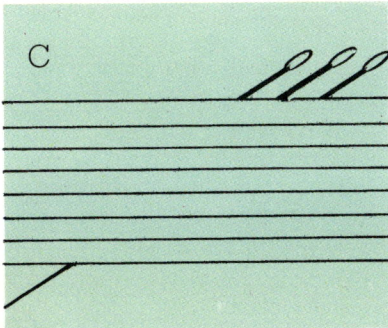

A

C

Eye test

Whose eyes?

A
B
C

 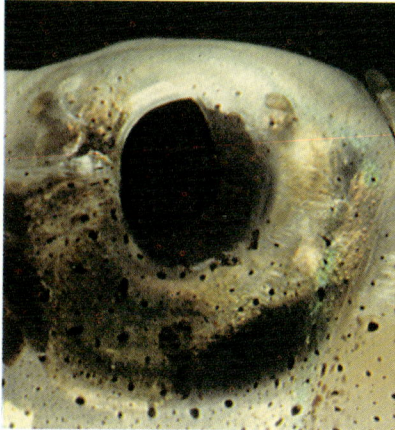 

▲ Which animal does each of these eyes belong to?

True or false

1. In dim light your pupils get smaller.
2. Refraction describes the bending of light.
3. Oil birds are blind.
4. Insects cannot see ultra-violet light.
5. The horned-toad squirts blood from its eyes.
6. Bright light contains small numbers of photons.
7. Octopuses have good colour vision.
8. Some deep-sea fish have lights to help them see.
9. Owls have good binocular vision.
10. A scallop may have as many as 200 eyes.
11. A frog can pull its eyes into its mouth.
12. Whales have tear glands.
13. You can anger a bull by showing it a red rag.

Your eyes

1. Name the sockets in which your eyeballs fit.
2. What do you use to move your eyes from side to side?
3. What do you call the transparent cover over the front of each eye?
4. Name the part of your eye which controls the amount of light entering?
5. What part of your eye focuses light onto the retina?
6. Name the two types of nerve cells found in your retina.
7. Name the part of the retina where you see most clearly.
8. Name the part of the retina where no image is formed.
9. What do tears do?

▲ Name this animal.

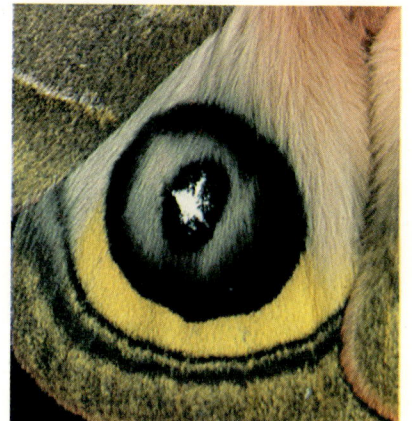

▲ Can you identify this picture?

Reflection puzzles

Suzannah took this photograph of her school clock tower reflected in a puddle. She kept notes of all the photographs she took. Here is what she wrote about this one.

Date photo taken June 15th. Time 5.45 pm. Exposure 1/60 sec at f/8.

Suzannah's watch keeps perfect time. So here is the puzzle! Was Suzannah's school clock fast or slow? By how much?

Sara is sitting in front of her dressing table mirror in her bedroom one afternoon. Her mother calls up from downstairs. 'We must leave for the station in five minutes'.

What time do you think Sara and her mother leave the house?

◀Which animal's eyes see the world like this? What do you think this is a picture of?

Mixed bag

1. Which animal has the biggest eyes?
2. Name the seven colours of the visible spectrum (rainbow).
3. Name the reflecting layer at the back of a cat's eyes.
4. What kind of vision does an animal have when both eyes face forwards?
5. Why do turtles cry?
6. Describe the shape of the front of a fish's eye.
7. Which bird uses its wings like an umbrella when fishing?
8. What are the three primary colours of light?
9. What are pit organs?

▲ Is this top hat taller than the width of the brim or vice versa?

Answers

Answers to questions in book

p 6: A piece of coal looks black because it absorbs all the wavelengths of light. No light is reflected.

p 6: It takes sunlight just over 8 minutes to reach the Earth's surface from the Sun.

p 15: Your pupils would quickly become smaller so that less light would enter the eyes.

p 17: A driver waiting at the traffic lights probably won't have a problem even if red/green colour blind. The driver knows by experience where the red and green lights are positioned.

p 22: There are at least five changes, which show the legs have moved.

p 27: The bottom photograph shows a predator — the pike. It feeds on fish like the perch shown in the top photograph.

p 32: The large eyes with their big pupils tell you that most owls are nocturnal birds.

p 46: The eyes of the hatchet fish look upwards towards the light coming from above. It can see its prey above it more easily.

p 48: When you turn the page upside down, the butterfly looks like an owl's face.

p 54-55

A. No, they are parallel. They seem to bend.

B. Yes, the square is really a square and the circle is really a circle. Their shapes are distorted by the radiating lines and the circle on the outside.

C. The needle on the right.

D. No, both lines are the same length.

E. Both lines are the same length.

You should see a picture of the Mona Lisa. If you have difficulty, try closing your eyes after looking at a piece of white paper.

Answers to quiz

Whose eyes:
A. Insect, B. Squid, C. Gecko

True or false:
1. false, 2. true, 3. false, 4. false, 5. true, 6. false, 7. false, 8. true, 9. true, 10. true, 11. true, 12. false, 13. false

Your eyes:
1. orbits, 2. muscles, 3. cornea, 4. iris, 5. lens, 6. rods and cones, 7. fovea, 8. blind spot, 9. keep the surface of the eye moist and kill germs.

Name this animal:
False-eyed frog.

Can you identify this picture:
Close up of eyespot on moth wing.

Reflection puzzles:
Suzannah's school clock was 5 minutes fast. Sara and her mother left the house at 2.55 pm.

An insect's eyes. It is a picture of some flowers.

Mixed bag:
1. giant squid, 2. red, orange, yellow, green, blue, indigo, violet, 3. tapetum, 4. binocular vision, 5. to get rid of salt which they do not want, 6. flat, 7. black heron, 8. red, green and blue, 9. the sensitive structures on the head of some snakes which help to pick up infra-red heat signals.

Optical illusions:
the height of the hat and the width of the brim are the same.

Glossary

binocular vision: seeing one image when looking at an object with both eyes.

bipolar cell: a special kind of cell in the retina which receives signals from small groups of cones.

blind spot: a small area at the back of the eye where there are no nerve cells.

colour blind: not able to tell the difference between some colours, e.g. red and green. 'Colour blind' is also used to describe animals that have no colour vision.

compound eye: a type of eye found in insects and crabs. It is made up of many small pieces.

cone: a special cell in the retina which is sensitive to colour and used for daylight vision.

cornea: the transparent cover in front of the eye.

eyeshine: the reflection of light from an animal's eyes.

eyespot: a round pattern that looks like an eye. Often found on butterfly and moth wings and other animals such as fish.

eyestripe: a thin dark line which seems to run across an animal's eye to help disguise it.

field of vision: the area or space around an animal which its eye can see.

focus: to produce a sharp, clear image. The lens in the eye focuses light onto the retina.

fovea: the small area of the retina where daylight vision is sharpest. It contains only cones.

image: the picture formed on the retina by light passing through the lens.

infra-red: the spectrum just beyond red light. It can be felt as heat.

iris: the coloured part of the eye between the cornea and the lens. It controls the amount of light entering the eye.

lens: the transparent part of the eye which focuses light onto the retina.

nictitating membrane: the third eyelid found in some animals. It can be pulled across the surface of the eye to give more protection.

photon: a unit of light energy.

pit organ: a heat-sensitive structure found in some snakes. It helps the snake to 'see' infra-red light.

polarized light: light in which the wavelengths vibrate in only one plane.

primary colour: one of three colours which, when mixed, can produce any other colour. The primary colours of light are red, green and blue. A mixture of all three produces white light.

pupil: the hole in the centre of the iris in the eye of vertebrates. It can be made bigger or smaller.

reflection: what happens when a beam of light is turned back by a surface, e.g. the reflection of light in a mirror.

refraction: the way a ray of light is bent when it passes at an angle from a less dense to a denser medium, e.g. from air into water.

retina: the light-sensitive layer of cells at the back of the eye of vertebrates. It is made up of rods and cones.

rod: a special cell in the retina of vertebrate animals used for seeing in dim light.

sclera: the tough, outer protective cover of the eyeball. In front of the eye it is transparent and forms the cornea.

simple eye: a single cell or group of cells that can detect light.

tapetum: a mirror-like layer behind the retina of some vertebrates which reflects light back into the eye. It improves night vision.

ultraviolet light: the spectrum just beyond violet light. It is invisible to humans but some birds and insects can see it.

visible spectrum: the rainbow-coloured bands of light seen when white light is split up. The red wavelengths are the longest and the violet wavelengths the shortest.

Index

Acknowledgements

ARTISTS:

David Anstey; Steve Lings/Linden Artists; Mick Loates/Linden Artists; Alan Male/Linden Artists; Maurice Pledger/Linden Artist; Michelle Ross/Linden Artists; Helen Townson; David Webb/Linden Artists; BLA Publishing Limited

PHOTOGRAPHIC CREDITS:

t = top; b = bottom; c = centre; l = left; r = right.

COVER: Michael Fogden/OSF. 6 Eric Chrichton/Bruce Coleman Ltd. 7t E.A. Janes/NHPA. 7b P. Davey/Frank Lane. 8t James Carmichael Jr./NHPA. 8b Stephen Dalton/NHPA. 9t Peter David/Frank Lane. 9b Dieter and Mary Page/Survival Anglia. 10l Hans Reinhard/Bruce Coltman Ltd. 10r Alfred Pasieka/Bruce Coleman Ltd. 11t Stephen Dalton/NHPA. 11b Robert A. Tyrrell/OSF. 12 Frieder Sauer/Bruce Coleman Ltd. 13t Mike Salisbury/Seaphot. 13b John Lythgoe/Seaphot. 15tl, tr and b Trevor Hill. 17 BLA Publishing Ltd. 18 Frank W. Lane/Frank Lane. 19t Otto Rogge/NHPA. 19b Zig Leszczynski/Animals Animals/OSF. 20 Animals Unlimited. 21t Dick Clarke/Seaphot. 21b L. West/Frank Lane. 22 David Maitland/Seaphot. 23 Tom and Pam Gardner/Frank Lane. 24t Stephen Dalton/NHPA. 24b Peter Johnson/NHPA. Jonathon Scott/Seaphot. 26t Melvin Grey/NHPA. 26b Franz J. Camenzind/Seaphot. 27t Jeff Goodman/NHPA. 27b Kenneth Lucas/Seaphot. 28 W. Rohdich/Frank Lane. 29 L. Campbell/NHPA. 30t Ron Austing/Frank Lane. 30b Michael Fogden/OSF. 31t Michael Fogden/OSF. 31b R. Teede/G.S.F. Picture Library. 32 Melvin Grey/NHPA. 34 Francisco Futil/Bruce Coleman Ltd. 35 Rod Williams/Bruce Coleman Ltd. 36 Michael Fogden/Bruce Coleman Ltd. 37 Kim Taylor/Bruce Coleman Ltd. 39 Bruce Davidson/Survival Anglia. 40 G.I. Bernard/NHPA. 42t Alex Kerstitch/Seaphot. 42b Peter Scoones/Seaphot. 44t Leo Collier/Seaphot. 44b Peter Scoones/Seaphot. 45t Frank Lane. 45b Stephen Dalton/NHPA. 46 Ken Lucas/Seaphot. 48 Peter Ward/Bruce Coleman Ltd. 49 Frank W. Lane/Frank Lane. 50t Frank Lane. 50b Walter Deas/Seaphot. 51t Michael Fogden/OSF. 51b Kathie Atkinson/OSF.